Learning Tree
1 2 3

Day and Night

By Susan Baker

Illustrated by Bernard Robinson

CHERRYTREE BOOKS

Read this book and see if you can do the experiments and answer the questions. Ask an adult or an older friend to tell you if your answers are right or to help you if you find the questions difficult. Often there is more than one answer to a question.

A Cherrytree Book

Designed and produced by
A S Publishing

First published 1990
by Cherrytree Press Ltd
a subsidiary of
The Chivers Company Ltd
Windsor Bridge Road
Bath, Avon BA2 3AX

Copyright © Cherrytree Press Ltd 1990

British Library Cataloguing in Publication Data
Baker, Susan,
    Day and night.
    1. Day & night.
    I. Title   II. Robinson, Bernard   III. Series
    529.2

    ISBN 0-7451-5092-6
Printed and bound in Italy by L.E.G.O. s.p.a., Vicenza

It is morning. It is time for you to get up.
Morning is the beginning of a new day.
The sun gets up in the morning.

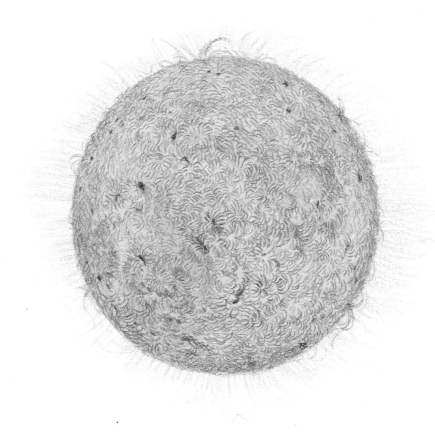

The sun is very hot and very bright.
It heats the earth and makes it light.
Never stare directly at the sun.
The bright light can damage your eyes.

The sun rises at dawn before most of us get up.
It peeps over the edge of the land and makes
the sky grow light.
All through the morning it moves across the sky.
It climbs higher and higher.

dawn

morning

mid-day

sunset

At mid-day the sun is high overhead.
Mid-day is sometimes called noon.

The sun goes on moving all through the
afternoon.
It sinks lower and lower in the sky.

As the sun sinks, the sky grows darker.
In the evening the sun sets.
It sinks below the land and darkness falls.

At night there is no light from the sun.
The only light comes from the moon and stars.

The sun is a star.
All the stars are hot and bright.
Our sun seems bigger and hotter than the
other stars because it is nearer to us.

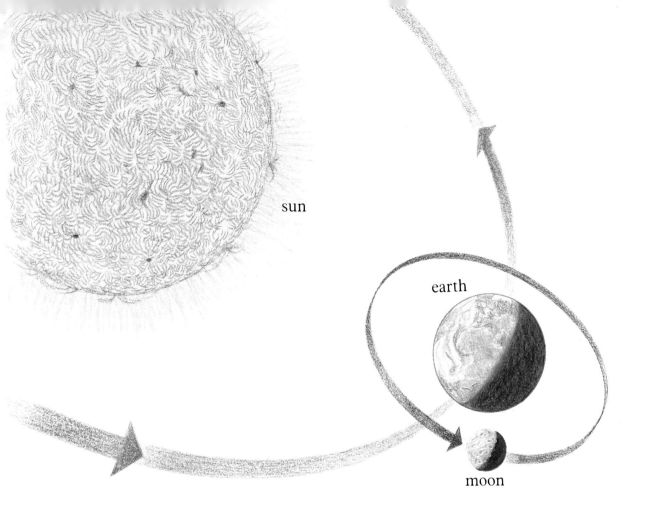

sun

earth

moon

The earth is a planet.
It travels round and round the sun.

The moon is a ball of rock that travels round
and round the earth.

9

As the earth goes round the sun, it spins.

Imagine a globe spinning in front of a lamp.
One half faces the lamp and is brightly lit.
As the globe turns, that half moves into the
darkness.
The other side moves into the light.

dawn

mid-day

afternoon

night

As the earth spins, light from the sun falls on one side of it.

It is day on that side of the world.

The other half of the world is in darkness.

It is night on that side of the earth.

11

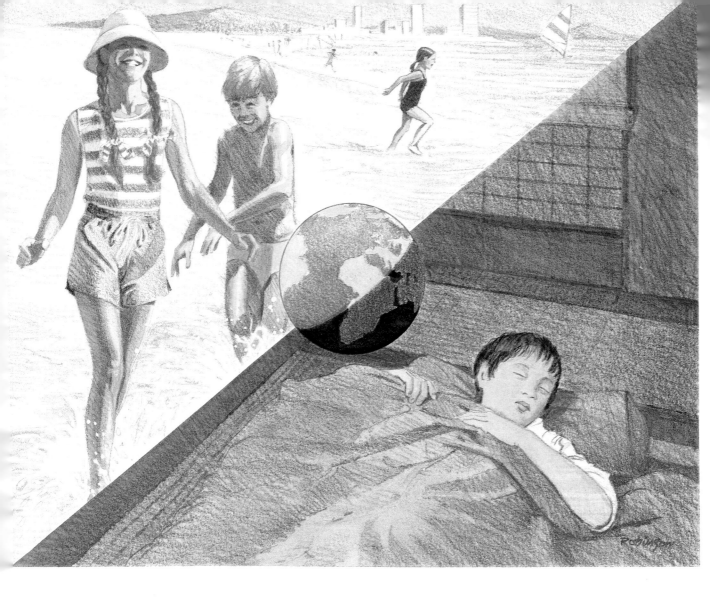

As the earth turns, the half that was in darkness moves into the light and day begins.

When you are getting up, people on the other side of the world are going to bed.

13

It takes 24 hours for the earth to turn.
A complete day lasts 24 hours.

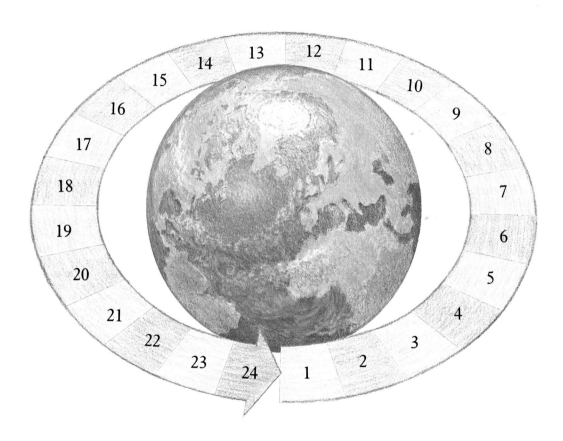

We call the time when it is light daytime.
We call the time when it is dark nighttime.

Most people work by day and sleep by night.
But some people work through the night.
They see by electric light.

Some animals sleep during the day and hunt
for food at night.
They can see better than we can in the dark.

As well as spinning round like a top, the earth also moves in a circle.

Put a ball in the middle of a space.
Pretend it is the sun and you are the earth.
Twirl round and round and move in a circle round the ball at the same time.
Try not to get giddy.

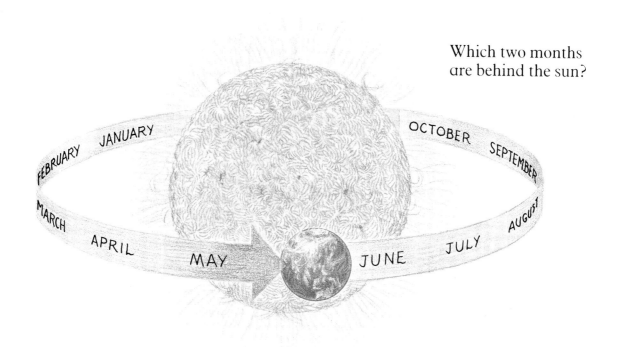

Which two months are behind the sun?

Does it take you longer to turn once or to circle all the way round the ball?
It takes the earth much longer.
It takes a whole year for it to go round the sun.

There are just over 365 days in a year.
This means that the earth spins 365 times in
its journey round the sun.

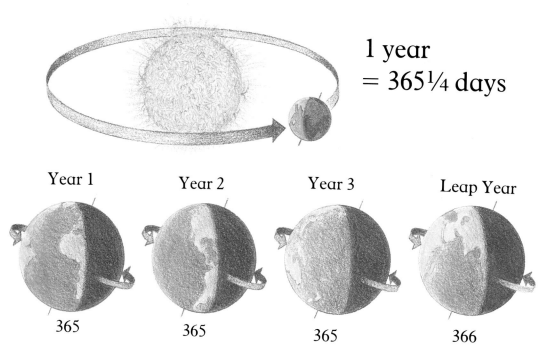

1 year
= 365¼ days

Year 1   Year 2   Year 3   Leap Year

365   365   365   366

In fact its journey takes exactly 365¼ days.
What happens to the quarter of a day?
Every four years we use up the four quarters
by having an extra day.
A year with an extra day is called a leap year.

The moon takes 29½ days to go round the earth.
We call about that time a month.
The moon has no light of its own.
We can only see it when the sun shines on it.
Sometimes it shines on only part of it.

You can tell the time by the sun.
You can make your own clock by watching the
shadows that the sun makes.

Borrow a watch and find a straight stick.
Push the stick into the ground and draw a
circle round it.
Every hour mark where the stick's shadow falls.
Next day you will not need the watch.
You can tell the time with your sundial.

More about day and night

The sun gives the world light and heat. Without the sun, the earth would have no life on it. But the sun can be dangerous. You need glasses with special filters before you can look at the sun. Never look directly at the sun with your naked eye or through a telescope.

Sunrise
Have you ever watched the sun rise? Try to get up early enough one day to see the dawn. It is best to see it in the open countryside or at sea where you can see the edge of the land — the horizon.

Seasons
Have you noticed that 'days' are longer in the summer than in the winter? The sun shines for more hours in the day during the summer. This is because of the changing seasons.

We have different seasons because of the way the earth spins. The earth is not upright but tilted at an angle. This means that the side tilted towards the sun gets more sun each day than the other side does. When it is summer on one side of the world, it is winter on the other. It is spring or autumn in between.

Equator
The equator is an imaginary line that goes right round the middle of the world. At the equator the sun shines for twelve hours every day, and there are twelve hours of night. There are no seasons. It is always hot.

Months
It takes the moon $29\frac{1}{2}$ days to go round the earth. Months last between 28 and 31 days. Remember this rhyme:
Thirty days hath September,
April, June and November.
All the rest have thirty-one,
Excepting February, that's clear.
Has twenty-eight,
And twenty-nine in each leap year.

1

1 Was it light or dark when you got up this morning?

2 Is it always dark when you go to bed?

3 What can hurt your eyes?

4 Which makes you feel hotter: sunlight or moonlight?

5 How many days are there in a week? What are the days called?

6 Can you read the sundial in the picture? What time of day is it?

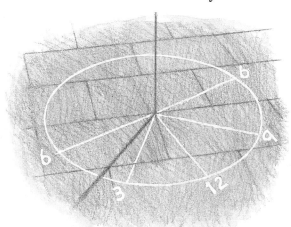

2

7 It is a good idea to keep a notebook. Write your answers in it and any questions you want to ask. Write down things about the sun and earth that you want to remember.

8 Which season is it now? Which season is it on the other side of the world?

9 Which are the two days of the weekend?

10 On fine days you can look out for shadows. At what time of day are shadows shortest? When are they longest?

11 At what time is the sun overhead?

12 Do you know the names of three animals that go out at night and sleep by day?

13 Draw a picture of an animal that hunts at night.

22

3

14 Why does the sun look bigger to us than other stars?

15 Does the sun really move across the sky?

16 How many hours does it take for the earth to go once round the sun?

17 Is it always dawn somewhere in the world?

18 If you were born on February 29, how old would you be the next time it was February 29?

19 Find out the name of the country on the opposite side of the world. You can look for it on a globe. Learn about the way people live there.

20 Which is usually hotter, morning or afternoon?

21 Where is the sun at midnight?

22 The moon is only a quarter of the size of the earth. Why do you think it sometimes looks as big as the sun?

23 The moon is a slightly different shape every night. Do you know why?

24 When the moon is fully lit by the sun, it is called a full moon or new moon. What are the other phases of the moon called?

25 What stops us seeing the sun properly on some days?

26 What does the word astronomy mean?

27 Find out what an eclipse is. Look in a dictionary or an astronomy book.

28 What does the word nocturnal mean?

29 Can you think of two reasons why we may sometimes not be able to see the moon?

Index

1 2 3 22, 23
24 hours 14
29½ days 19
365 days 18
365¼ days 18
afternoon 11
autumn 21
brightness 4, 8
clock 20
damage to eyes 4, 21
darkness 7, 10, 11, 12, 14, 15
dawn 5, 11, 21
day 3, 11, 12, 14, 15, 18, 19, 21
daytime 14
earth 4, 9, 10, 11, 12, 14, 16, 17, 21
electric light 15
equator 21
getting up 3, 5, 13, 21
globe 10
going to bed 13
heat 4, 8, 21
horizon 21
hours 14, 21
land 5, 21
leap year 18
life 21
light 4, 7, 10, 11, 14, 15, 19, 21

mid-day 6, 11
months 17, 19, 21
moon 7, 9, 19
morning 3, 5
movement of the earth 9, 10, 16, 17, 18
night 7, 11, 15
nighttime 14
noon 6
planet 9
seasons 21
shadows 20
sky 5, 6, 7
sleep 15
spinning earth 10, 11, 16, 17, 18, 21
spring 21
stars 7, 8
summer 21
sun 3-11, 16-21
sundial 20
sunrise 5, 21
sunset 6, 7
time 14, 20
winter 21
year 17, 18